Revised Edition

Sweet Memories of Christmas Cookbook

Patricia B. Mitchell

Copyright © 1989, 1991 by Patricia B. Mitchell.

This book was entitled **Christmas: How Sweet It Is!...** *through its first edition and the first three printings of this revised edition.*

Published 1991 by the author.
  Mail: Mitchells, Box 429, Chatham, VA 24531
  Book Sales: 800-967-2867
  E-mail: Answers@FoodHistory.com
  Websites: FoodHistory.com and
       MitchellsPublications.com

Printed in the U. S. A.
ISBN-10: 0-925117-48-X
ISBN-13: 978-0-925117-48-9

Sixth Printing, December 2007

- *Illustrations* -

Front cover silhouette - adapted from illustration by Arthur Nelson in P. O. Bersell, "What Christmas Means to Me," in Randolph E. Haugan, ed., **Christmas: An American Annual of Christmas Literature & Art,** *Vol. 5, Augsburg Publishing House, Minneapolis, Minnesota, 1935, p. 15.*

All other illustrations - adapted from images provided by Dover Publications, Inc., New York.

Table of Contents

Introduction..1
Rocky Mountain Cake...2
Angel Curl Coconut Cake..3
Four-Day Carroll County Coconut Cake....................4
Mama's Icebox Fruitcake..5
Japanese Fruitcake..7
Christmastide Pumpkin Crunch...............................8
Winter Dream Sour Cream Banana Pudding...............9
Mava's Marvelous Lemon Pound Cake.....................9
Twelfth Night Cake..10
Aunt Lena's Raisin Cake.......................................12
Stollen..13
Helen's Heavenly Chocolate Cake..........................15
Best Ever Brownies..16
"Joan's-on-the-Other-Side-of-the-World" Mincemeat....17
Effie's Damson Pie..18
Papa Noel's Pumpkin Pie......................................19
Mama Marie's Sweet Potato Pie.............................19
Microwave Sweet Potato Soufflé............................20
Sweet Memories Holiday Fudge.............................23
Mary's Candied Grapefruit Peel.............................23
Chocolate-Covered Mounds..................................25
Chocolate Nut Balls...26
Molasses Taffy...28
"Visions of Sugar Plums" Nut Roll.........................30
Home for the Holidays Christmas Strawberries...........32
Peanut Butter Candy..33
Marie Wells's Date Roll..35
Holiday World Date Swirls...................................35
Grandma's Cookies..36
Chocolate Nut-Crackle Sauce.................................37

* * * * * * * * * * * * *

Introduction

Sweet Memories of Christmas and its companion volume **Coming Home for Christmas Cookbook** are unusual in that the information upon which they are based was collected by means of a Christmas questionnaire which I sent out to over one hundred friends and relatives. Responses to the questionnaire provided me with much of the background information for the recipes. Many of the recipes are also printed courtesy of the survey respondents.

One thing which I quickly learned from my survey is that while people happily eat turkey and "all the trimmings" at Christmas, when asked to name favorite holiday foods, the majority of individuals list dessert and particular fruits as being their favorites.

I sent questionnaires to folks scattered all over the United States, but because I'm a Southerner and most of my relatives live in the South, many of the answers came from the South. One fact that the survey demonstrated indisputably: coconut cake is the most frequently served Christmas dessert in this region. Second choice? You guessed it: fruitcake!

Read on to discover more fascinating regional food patterns and customs, and to see where your culinary holiday traditions fit in. (Regional? Rural? Ethnic? Unique?) And be sure to try lots of the recipes. "Sweet memories!"

* * * * * * * * * * * * *

Rocky Mountain Cake

Frances Hallam Hurt of Chatham, Virginia (but raised in Dallas, Texas) gives easy instructions for this recipe: "Yellow cake batter/layers. 7-minute icing. Soak preserved fruit & nuts a week in spirits (bourbon, brandy) in tightly sealed jar. Mix half of icing with half fruit to go between layers. Spread fruit on top, then icing on top of it & on sides. Slather with coconut. I eat most of it myself."

Some Rocky Mountain Cake specialists do not soak the fruits and nuts, as you will see in the following "made from scratch" recipe from Gertrude Jones of Chatham. She uses nuts, raisins, figs, candied cherries and pineapple, and coconut. Some local cooks utilize currants and dates in place of the candied fruit, but the cherries look mighty pretty for Christmas!

Ruth Hammer, who grew up in the early part of the century in Amelia County, Virginia, put Rocky Mountain Cake in the context of a typical Christmas menu from her childhood: turkey, stuffing and gravy, cranberry salad, celery, yams, mince pie, Rocky Mountain Cake, and fruitcake.

* * *

1 c. soft shortening (half butter)
2 c. sugar
3 c. cake flour
4 tsp. baking powder
1 tsp. salt
1 1/3 c. thin milk (half water)
2 tsp. vanilla
6 egg whites (3/4 c.), stiffly beaten

Cream sugar and shortening together until fluffy. Sift flour, baking powder, and salt together. Stir alternately with milk and flavoring. Fold in egg whites.

Pour into well-greased and floured pans. Bake in 350° F. oven for 30 or 35 minutes.

Icing for Rocky Mountain Cake:

3 c. sugar
3/4 c. water
4 egg whites, stiffly beaten
1 c. chopped English walnuts or almonds
3 figs, chopped finely
1/2 c. chopped candied cherries
1/2 c. chopped candied pineapple
Coconut for outside

Boil sugar and water together until it spins a fine thread (236° F.) and pour slowly over stiffly-beaten egg whites, beating constantly until cool and of spreading consistency.

Save enough to ice the outside of the cake before mixing nuts, fruit, etc. Add remaining ingredients and blend well. Spread between layers. Decorate with raisins, walnuts, and cherries, after putting coconut over the cake. Makes enough for three 9-inch layers.

Angel Curl Coconut Cake

This recipe comes from Hattie Webb of Staunton, Virginia. — By the way, when the Beaver (my maiden name) family gets together for our annual Christmas reunion, someone always brings a big coconut cake. For years I heard discussions of how fantastic green coconut cake is and who should bring one the next year, and conversations about who made the best one, etc. Every year I looked for someone to bring in a green-tinted coconut cake. Always I saw white coconut cake. I kept waiting and watching; every reunion I anticipated that somebody would finally bring *it*. And then I learned that *green* coconut means (at least to Beavers) *fresh* coconut!

* * *

1 pkg. (2-layer size) yellow cake mix
1 pkg. (4-serving size) vanilla instant pudding
1 1/3 c. water
4 eggs
1/2 c. vegetable oil
2 c. shredded coconut
1 c. chopped walnuts or pecans

    In large mixer bowl, blend cake mix, pudding mix, water, eggs, and oil. Beat at medium speed of electric mixer 4 minutes. Stir in coconut and nuts. Pour into 3 greased and floured 9-inch pans. Bake at 350° F. for 35 minutes. Cool in pans 15 minutes, remove, and cool on rack. Fill and frost with coconut-cream cheese frosting:

4 tbsp. margarine
2 c. coconut
8-oz. pkg. cream cheese
2 tsp. milk
3 1/2 c. sifted confectioners' sugar
1/2 tsp. vanilla

    Melt 2 tbsp. margarine in a skillet. Add the coconut; stir constantly over low heat until golden brown. Spread coconut on paper towel to cool. Cream 2 tbsp. margarine with cream cheese. Add milk and sugar alternately, beating well. Add vanilla; stir in 1 3/4 c. of coconut. Spread on top and sides of cake layers. Sprinkle with remaining coconut.

Four-Day Carroll County Coconut Cake

    Helen Edwards Melton, my longtime friend of Hillsville, Virginia, provides me with many an outstanding recipe. The following entry is hers, as well as the sweetly nostalgic response to my question about her favorite Christmas remembered: "I could not select one; but as a child my Christmas centered around my grandparents. Their delight was for the children and grandchildren to return home and open gifts and share a meal."

* * *

2 c. sugar
2 c. sour cream
2 c. fresh coconut (you can use frozen)

    Stir the above together and leave in refrigerator overnight. The next day, make a white cake or use 1 box Duncan Hines White Cake Mix. When cool, split the layers.

    Put the mixture between the layers. Put this in the refrigerator and leave for four days before serving.

    Fresh coconut may be sprinkled over the slices when served.

Mama's Icebox Fruitcake

    At my childhood home in Dry Fork, Virginia, Christmas was also a time for many of the "clan" to visit, because my parents and I lived with my mother's father. On Christmas Day my Mom's brother Roy Jones and his family came for Christmas dinner, and frequently the two other brothers, Fred and Jake, and their families came in sometime during the holidays. (On an earlier Sunday in December my father's family, five Beaver brothers, had a Christmas reunion.)

    This was all great fun for me (not to mention the sheer joy of being out of school, and the excitement of receiving presents), but, no doubt, much extra work for Mom. — Holiday preparations began early, and at Thanksgiving Mom would recruit Dad to help with her Icebox Fruitcake. (That was before the day of packaged crumbs and pre-diced dried fruit.) Dad would break up vanilla wafers and graham crackers with a rolling pin and then pulverize them with his hands. They would chop fruit into a large, oval, white enameled dishpan. (They used that because it was big enough to contain all the ingredients for several cakes.) All this crumbling and chopping and mixing took hours, but the resulting fruit cake was worth "all the fuss." After the cake (or cakes) were made, Mom gave them a drink of sweet wine, or fruit juice, or brandy at least once a week until Christmas to keep the cake moist and to add "oomph". . . .

Nowadays part of the work is done for you, so go ahead and get out your dishpan!

* * *

1 box vanilla wafers, crushed
1 box graham crackers, crushed (or the equivalent amount of packaged graham cracker crumbs)
1 c. candied red cherries
1 box white raisins
1 box dark raisins
2 pkg. figs, chopped
2 pkg. dates, chopped
2 c. mixed nuts (pecans, Brazil nuts, English walnuts)

1 lg. bag marshmallows
1 can Eagle Brand condensed milk

Note: Save out some cherry and nut halves to decorate the top of the cake.

Combine the first eight ingredients. Meanwhile, in a double boiler, melt the marshmallows into the condensed milk. Add this mixture into the dry ingredients, a little at a time, until moist. Pack this mixture into a cake mold lined with wax paper. Arrange the extra cherries and nuts on top of the cake in a pretty pattern. Wrap well with plastic wrap, and store a few weeks in refrigerator before using.

Japanese Fruitcake

My Aunt Janette Forbes Beaver of Charlotte spoke about her mother's White Fruitcake and an aunt's Japanese Fruitcake. When I wrote Aunt Jan requesting the latter recipe, she graciously sent it to me, commenting, "I get increased saliva thinking about [Japanese Fruitcake]."

* * *

1 c. butter
1 c. sugar
Yolks of 6 eggs, or 4 whole eggs
1 c. sweet milk
1 tsp. salt
1 tsp. vanilla
1 tsp. lemon extract

4 c. flour
1 tsp. baking powder
1 tsp. cinnamon
1 tsp. cloves
1 tsp. allspice
1 c. ground raisins

Beat together the first seven ingredients. In a separate bowl, mix thoroughly the remaining ingredients. Combine both mixtures, and pour into three greased and floured cake pans. Bake at 350° F. for around 20 minutes or until done.

Meanwhile make **filling:**

2 c. sugar
1 c. water
2 c. grated coconut
1 c. crushed pineapple
1 c. ground raisins
Grated rind of 2 oranges
Grated rind of 2 lemons

Mix ingredients together, spread on layers; then stack the layers.

Christmastide Pumpkin Crunch

Aunt Jan also contributed the following recipe. These dessert squares can be prepared far in advance because they keep extremely well when refrigerated.

* * *

1 16-oz. can pumpkin
1 large can evaporated milk
1 c. sugar
3 eggs
1/2 tsp. cinnamon
1 box yellow cake mix
1 c. chopped nuts
2 sticks butter or margarine, melted

Preheat oven to 350° F. Line 9x13x2-inch pan with waxed paper. Mix pumpkin, evaporated milk, sugar, eggs, and cinnamon together and pour into pan. Top with 1 box dry cake mix, and pat nuts over mixture evenly. Pour melted margarine over nuts evenly. Bake at 350° F. for 50-60 minutes.

Invert and peel off wax paper. Mix **frosting** ingredients:

1 lg. pkg. (8 oz.) cream cheese
3/4 c. Cool Whip (thawed)
1/2 c. powdered sugar

Frost cake and refrigerate.

Winter Dream Sour Cream Banana Pudding

My cousin Kathy Beaver Marlow gets credit for the following rich and easy recipe.

* * *

3 small pkg. vanilla pudding mix
5 c. milk
1 carton sour cream
1 large carton Cool Whip, divided in half

Vanilla wafers
Bananas

Combine the first four ingredients. In a glass (or pyrex) dish make layers of vanilla wafers, sliced bananas, and the pudding mixture. Top with remainder of Cool Whip.

Mava's Marvelous Lemon Pound Cake

On the Sunday following Christmas Day my family and I would drive to Martinsville, Virginia, to eat a mega-meal with Uncle Roy and Aunt Ethel Jones and my cousins. I remember the bustle of greetings at the door, and then I recall how I'd scoot through the living room to stand on the hall heat register. (I'd be dressed in a Sunday dress, and that billowing rush of heat felt oh, so welcome on cold legs!) Soon, though, Cousin Nelson (he's my age) and I would go tearing off to see some of his new toys.

Pretty soon we'd all fill our plates, buffet-style, and sit down to eat some of Aunt Ethel's plate-scrapingly delicious food. — My favorite part, though was dessert. There would be several pies and cakes from which to choose, but my choice was Aunt Ethel's pound cake, a rich, honest, uncomplicated cake. (The recipe is found in my *Simply Scrumptious Southern Sweets*.) The following marvelous pound cake is almost identical, except that rather than using vanilla, Mava Vass (of Hillsville, Virginia) uses lemon flavoring. That refreshing zing makes Mava's Marvelous Lemon Pound Cake a perfect ending to a bountiful Christmas feast.

* * *

1 stick margarine
1 c. Crisco
2 2/3 c. sugar
3 c. flour
1/2 tsp. salt
1 c. milk

    Place all ingredients in mixer and mix until light and fluffy. After mixing, add:

1 tsp. baking powder
3 tsp. lemon flavoring

Then add, one at a time:

5 eggs

Mix well. Bake at 325° F. for 60-90 minutes, checking on doneness.

Twelfth Night Cake

    In New Orleans on January 6th (the twelfth day after Christmas), King's Day or Epiphany is celebrated. This commemorates the visit of the Wise Men to Bethlehem. It is sometimes known as *Le Petit Noël*. In the old days, among Creole society, an immense cake was served at a party. A bean (symbolizing wisdom) or perhaps a ring (representing faithfulness) was baked in the cake. The individual who happened to be served the slice of cake containing the trinket had the honor of being "king" or "queen" for a week, and the responsibility of bringing the King's Cake to the next "selection" party. (New royalty was chosen each week up to Mardi Gras.)

Other objects can also be baked into such a cake. These things supposedly symbolize certain characteristics which will be evident in the person who gets that particular item in his or her piece of cake. The list reads like this:

A dried pea — *also showing wisdom;*
A button — *also representing faithfulness;*
A whole clove — *humor; the "court jester;"*
A dime — *wealth;*
A thimble — *patience;*
A heart shape — *devotion.*

At Christmastime in Finland an almond is baked into rice pudding — "luck" for the finder. Other holiday meal menu items in Finland? — Roast suckling pig; ham baked in a rye-dough crust, and served with turnip pudding.

Following is a version of Twelfth Night Cake found in *The Picayune's Creole Cook Book (Second Edition)*, originally published by the *Picayune* daily newspaper in New Orleans in 1901.

* * *

2 lbs. of the best flour (use 1 1/2 lbs. initially)
1/2 oz. baking yeast, dissolved in a little warm water
Milk or water
1/2 lb. flour
1/2 oz. salt
6-12 eggs, beaten
1 c. sugar
1 lb. butter

Put 1 1/2 lbs. of the flour into a large mixing bowl. Add the softened yeast, and gradually mix in enough milk or water to make a fairly soft, workable dough. Knead until smooth. Cover. Let rise until double in bulk. Next add the remaining 1/2 lb. flour and the salt. Then stir in the six eggs which have been beaten with the sugar and butter. (Add more eggs if the batter is stiff.) Knead briefly. Let rise. Knead gently and form into a large ring, leaving a hole in the center. Pat and flatten a little. Place on a baking pan lined with a buttered sheet of paper. Cover and let rise an hour.

Glaze dough with a beaten egg. Bake at 350° F. until done. Decorate with dragées, caramels, etc.

Aunt Lena's Raisin Cake

My New Orleans friend Sister Olivia Wassmer, O. S. C., shared with me her monastery's recipe booklet (*Sampler Cookbook*, © 1990 St. Clare's Monastery, New Orleans). Sister Olivia contributed the following recipe. (She is a multi-talented lady: a skilled artist, printer, and she even plays the piano at the famous Beauregard-Keyes House Christmas party.)

* * *

1 1/2 c. sugar
1 c. cooking oil
3 eggs, well-beaten
2 c. sifted flour
1 tsp. baking soda
1 tsp. salt
1 tsp. allspice
1 tsp. cinnamon
1 tsp. nutmeg
1 c. buttermilk
1 tsp. vanilla
1 c. raisins (or finely chopped prunes)
1/2 c. chopped nuts

Preheat oven to 350° F. Grease one 9x12-inch pan. Blend sugar, oil, and eggs. Mix well until eggs are lemon-colored. Combine dry ingredients. Add dry mixture and buttermilk alternately to sugar, oil, and egg mixture, beginning and ending with dry mixture. Add vanilla, raisins, and nuts, and mix well. Bake in a 9x12-inch greased pan at 350° F. for 40-45 minutes. Let cool 15 minutes before pouring sauce over cake. (Leave cake in pan.)

Sauce:

1 c. sugar
1/2 c. buttermilk
1/2 tsp. baking soda
1 tbsp. corn syrup
1/2 c. butter
1/2 tsp. vanilla

Mix and boil all ingredients for 3 minutes. Use a large pot because it bubbles up. Without beating it, pour it hot over the cake. Let stand until cool before cutting cake.

Serves 15. Serve in pan.

Stollen

Margot Richter Mayhew, my good friend and sister in Christ, lives near Gretna, Virginia, now, but she came to the United States in 1962 from her native state of Hesse, in (then West) Germany. Margot filled out a Christmas survey for me and also submitted several Christmas-type recipes. Both she and Curtis Whitehead of Chatham, Virginia, gave me recipes for stollen, a German Christmas bread. The two recipes for this traditional sweet bread were strikingly similar. — Margot tells me that she often deletes the citrus rind, nuts, and candied fruits (using raisins, because her children prefer it that way). Since it is a sweet bread, stollen is not served as we would present a dessert cake, at the end of a meal. Instead, Margot comments, it can be offered as a refreshment on Christmas Eve, for breakfast on Christmas morning, or at *kaffeezeit* ("coffeetime," daily, between 3 and 4 p.m.) on Christmas Day and New Year's Day.

The following version is the one given me by Curtis Whitehead, who obtained it from her German daughter-in-law, Simone Jacoby Whitehead.

* * *

1 c. milk
1 c. melted butter or margarine
1/2 c. water
5 1/4 c. all-purpose flour
1/4 c. sugar
1 tsp. salt
2 pkg. active dry yeast
2 eggs, beaten
1/2 tsp. grated lemon rind
1/2 tsp. grated orange rind
1/2 c. seedless raisins
1/2 c. chopped candied fruit
1/2 c. chopped nuts
3 tbsp. butter or margarine, softened
1/2 c. sugar
1 tbsp. ground cinnamon
1 1/2 c. powdered sugar
2 to 3 tbsp. water or milk
1/4 tsp. vanilla extract
Candied fruit and nuts for decorating

Combine milk, 1 c. melted butter and 1/2 c. water in a small saucepan; place over low heat just until lukewarm.

Combine flour, 1/4 c. sugar, salt, and yeast in a large mixing bowl; stir in warm milk mixture and eggs, mixing well. Add lemon and orange rind, raisins, fruit, and nuts; mix well. Cover dough, and let rise to double.

Divide dough in half; roll each piece into an oval about 1/2 inch thick. Spread with softened butter. Combine 1/2 c. sugar and cinnamon; sprinkle over butter. Fold over almost in half, so that the bottom edge extends slightly beyond the top. Press slightly on *folded* edge to help stollen hold shape when rising. Transfer stollens to baking sheets and let rise in a warm place (about 85 degrees) until double. Bake at 350° F. for 25 minutes or until golden brown.

Combine powdered sugar, water or milk, and vanilla; drizzle over warm stollens. Decorate with candied fruit and nuts. Yield: 2 stollens.

Helen's Heavenly Chocolate Cake

Just as pound cake is an oft-enjoyed Christmas treat (and a year-round reliable dessert idea), chocolate cake was listed on my surveys as frequently appearing on the holiday table. In fact, Christmas, like Valentine's Day, is a prime time sampling opportunity for chocoholics with many questionnaire respondents listing chocolate "something" as their favorite holiday food. Chocolate pound cake, chocolate layer cake, "Buckeyes" (peanut butter/chocolate balls), "Turtles" (caramel/pecan/ chocolate candy), Red Velvet Cake, fudge, and chocolate Santas were all (droolingly) recorded. — One person wrote on her questionnaire that she left candy, cookies, and hot chocolate out for St. Nick. (Presumably her parents told her that the jolly old man came *very* quickly after she went to bed. — Have you ever pulled the "skin" off the top of cool hot chocolate?)

Here, for all chocolate devotees, is a "keeper-of-a-recipe," given to Helen Melton by her Aunt Anna Lee Sizemore of Galax, Virginia.

* * *

1 c. butter or margarine
2 1/2 c. sugar
2 eggs, unbeaten
3 c. flour
1/4 tsp. salt
2 tbsp. cocoa
2 tbsp. vanilla

2 c. buttermilk
2 tsp. baking soda

    Cream butter, add sugar, and continue beating. Add eggs, one at a time, and beat well after each. Add milk and dry ingredients alternately. Bake in greased and floured 8-inch layer pans at 350° F. for 25 minutes or until done. When cooled, top with the following "whipped-cream" icing:

3 tbsp. flour
1 c. butter, margarine, or shortening
1 tsp. vanilla
1 c. milk
1 c. granulated sugar

    Cook flour and milk on low heat until thick. Let flour mixture cool. Cream sugar, butter, and vanilla until fluffy. Add to flour mixture. Beat until mixture is like whipped cream. Spread on cake layers. Sprinkle with coconut or nuts if desired.

Best Ever Brownies

    This recipe is a recent creation of mine. Its more healthful ingredients will offset any Christmas dieting/guilt/ "I'd better weigh" thoughts that flit through your head.

* * *

2 c. whole wheat flour
2/3 c. carob powder
1/2 c. nonfat dry milk powder
1/2 tsp. baking soda
1/2 tsp. salt
2/3 c. sugar
1 c. chopped walnuts or pecans
2 lg. very ripe bananas
2 tsp. vanilla
1 1/2 c. buttermilk or sour milk

Mix the dry ingredients. In a separate bowl mix the liquids. Combine the mixtures. Stir together well. Pour the batter into a greased 7x11- or 9x13-inch pyrex dish and bake at 350° F. for 20-25 minutes.

"Joan's-On-the-Other-Side-of-the-World" Mincemeat

Joan Mitchell Keith, my sister-in-law, gave me her recipe for mincemeat. I had ample opportunity to taste and test her mincemeat back in 1969-70 because Henry and I "inherited" a large collection of jars of Joan's mincemeat when Joan and family moved to Ceylon (Sri Lanka). They could not take glass jars of food along, of course; and since they were not sure how long they would be gone, they gave Henry and me (we were just married) lots of their canned goods.

I was new to cooking but I learned to make crust for a mince pie; I experimented with mince cookies; I even tried it in vegetable soup made from leftovers. (I figured mince*meat* had *meat* in it, so maybe it would be good protein. — It definitely did not enhance the flavor of the soup; it would be accurate to say, though a bit of an understatement, that it dominated *detrimentally* the taste of the soup!) Nevertheless we still can appreciate mincemeat, so here is Joan's-on-the-Other-Side-of-the-World Mincemeat!

* * *

2 gal. green tomatoes, chopped
1/2 c. suet, chopped
Grated rind of 1 orange
1 lb. light brown sugar
1 lb. raisins
1/4 tsp. salt
1/2 tsp. allspice
1/2 tsp. cinnamon
1 qt. apples, peeled and chopped

Combine all ingredients. Bring to a rapid boil, and simmer until thickened. Pour into sterilized jars and seal.

Historical note: Mince pies date back a long time. In the 16th century the spices contained in mince pie were thought to symbolize the spices brought by the Wise Men to Baby Jesus. - There was a belief that if a person ate a mince pie (I hope they mean "tasted a mince pie") on each of the Twelve Days of Christmas, he or she would have twelve happy months in the new year. On Christmas Day, 1666, the diarist Samuel Pepys recorded that he got up earlier than his wife "who was desirous to sleep having sat up till four this morning seeing her mayds [maids] make mince pies."

Effie's Damson Pie

A family may have the habit or tradition of serving a certain food on a particular occasion. For this Beaver (that is my maiden name), damson pie has always been associated with Christmas. My father's stepmother, Effie, provided glistening sweet/tart damson plum pies for our annual Beaver Christmas reunions. Later on, when she was gone, others often brought damson pie. There is no "secret recipe." What you do is this: when damsons are ripe, cook them down with lots of sugar (damsons are rather sour) to a thick puree. Freeze in 2- or 3-cup portions. Come December, pour that filling into a single unbaked pie shell (or make however many pies you need), and bake until crust is nicely and lightly browned. Cool, and serve topped with whipped cream (if desired).

Papa Noel's Pumpkin Pie

Pumpkin Pie was listed as a favorite Noel dessert by Patrick Daily, Pittsburgh native. The following is an old-fashioned recipe from New Orleans.

* * *

2 c. mashed, stewed pumpkin
2 c. milk
3 tbsp. butter, melted
1/4 tsp. salt
4 eggs
1 c. sugar (more or less, to taste)
1/2 tsp. each of ground mace, cinnamon, and allspice
1 tbsp. brandy (optional)
Confectioners' sugar

Combine all ingredients (except confectioners' sugar). Pour mixture into three baked pie shells, and bake at 350° F. for 30 minutes, or until set. When cool, sprinkle lightly with confectioners' sugar.

Mama Marie's Sweet Potato Pie

Mrs. Marie Wells, our friend Stuart Wells's mother, contributed the next decidedly-Southern dessert smoothie. (And what smells or fragrances did son Stuart associate with Yuletide? The lush aroma of the bright, copper-colored custard, its flaky pastry, its spices? Why, no, although this and Marie's Date Roll are his two favored holiday foods. — He remembers resonant whiffs of their decorated fir tree, "and the smells of new perfumes that my mother usually got for a present.")

* * *

1 unbaked 9-inch pie shell
1 1/2 c. mashed cooked sweet potatoes

1 tsp. cinnamon
3/4 tsp. salt
1/2 tsp. allspice
1/4 tsp. mace
2 eggs, beaten
2 tbsp. butter or margarine, melted
1/2 c. firmly packed brown sugar
1 (14 1/2 - oz.) can undiluted evaporated milk

    Combine ingredients for pie filling and pour into pastry shell. Bake at 425° F. for 10 minutes, then reduce heat to 350° F. and bake for 25 minutes or until the filling is set.

Microwave Sweet Potato Soufflé

    From *Woodville Red Recipes* (© 1987 by Cookbook Publishers, Inc. of Olathe, KS for the Woodville Tabithas) comes my Mississippi friend Honey Gross's instructions for Microwave Sweet Potato Soufflé. (By the way, Honey lists ambrosia and coconut as her childhood Christmas dessert favorites.)

* * *

3 tbsp. flour
1/2 tsp. salt
1/2 c. sugar
1 c. evaporated milk
5 eggs, separated
4 tbsp. margarine
1 tsp. cinnamon
1/4 tsp. nutmeg
1 16-oz. can sweet potatoes, drained and mashed
3/4 tsp. cream of tartar
1/4 c. sugar

    In 2-quart batter bowl, combine flour, salt, and 1/2 cup sugar. Gradually blend in evaporated milk. Microwave at

100% power for 3 1/2 to 4 minutes, or until thick, but not dry. Stir halfway through cooking. Stir half of the hot mixture into well-beaten egg yolk; stir well. Return yolk mixture to remaining hot mixture, continuing to stir until blended. Add margarine, cinnamon and nutmeg. Microwave at 100% power for 1 minute. Stir in sweet potatoes. Set aside.

In 2-quart batter bowl, beat egg whites and cream of tartar at high speed until frothy. Gradually add 1/4 cup sugar and continue beating until stiff. With same beaters, beat sweet potato mixture until smooth. Using a gentle folding action, fold egg whites into potato mixture.

In 2-quart soufflé dish or a straight-sided dish that has a collar made from freezer paper, pour in mixture. Microwave at 70% power for 3 minutes. Turn dish. Microwave at 30% power for 10 to 12 minutes or until edges appear dry and firm. Serve immediately.

As far as the concept of using a Christmas tree is concerned, the tradition in this country dates back to the era of the Revolutionary War. Hessian soldiers are credited with having introduced children in Newport, Rhode Island to their first view of a Christmas tree (evergreens symbolized life to the Germans). By the mid-1800's German influence had spread the use of a decorated evergreen tree for the Christmas holidays throughout European-settled North America.

In response to the question about how long the tree was up, answers varied dramatically. Marcella Sillars, who grew up in Rib Falls, Wisconsin, reported that their tree was put up on December 24 and taken down in March. Other respondents erected their tree as early as the day after Thanksgiving and some took it down on December 26.

The Dutch brought the legend of "Sinter Klaas" to Colonial America. The idea of a jolly old Santa has its roots in the story of the life of a real person. History and time give a somewhat clouded view of this man, but it thought that he was a fourth-century bishop of Myra in Lycia on the coast of Asia Minor. The mythological tale explains that Saint Nicholas heard about a rich man who lost his fortune, and was contemplating sending his three daughters out onto the street as prostitutes. (Some versions just say that they could not marry because they had no dowries.) Nicholas supposedly crept to the window of their house on three successive nights and tossed a bag of gold into the room each night. One bag even landed in a slipper warming by the fire (some renditions say in a stocking hanging by the fire to dry). — Hundreds of years later, children in Europe were encouraged to put out shoes or stockings to receive gifts from Saint Nicholas. So you see how truth and fantasy became intertwined.

Holly is associated with the celebration of Christ's birth, too. (Prior to the Christian era, holly symbolized foresight to the Greeks, and goodwill and friendship to the Romans. The Native Americans believed that holly signified fierceness, courage, and eternal life.) — For Christians, the evergreen foliage symbolizes everlasting life; and, in some cultures, the red berries stand for the wounds and shed blood of our Savior.

When hubby Henry was growing up, he associated Christmas with annual candy binges. His mother made superlative fudge and candied grapefruit peel to keep on hand during December. (She did not normally prepare and keep candies around.) Henry remembers boxes and canisters of these confitures placed here and there, as well as containers of pecan-stuffed dates, and he recalls happily gorging himself. — Both Henry and his sister Joan connect the aroma of candied grapefruit peel with the holidays.

Many inquiry respondents do recollect certain smells as being distinctly "Christmas." Cakes, cookies, and pies baking; cinnamon; ginger; turkey; ham; oysters; sage; oranges and tangerines; chocolate; homemade yeast rolls; fruitcake; peppermint candy canes; and eggnog were some food smells listed. Non-food fragrances were pine trees (of various types); bayberry; fire in the fireplace; and scented candles.

Sweet Memories Holiday Fudge
(Henry's Mother's Recipe)

2 squares unsweetened chocolate, or 4-5 tbsp. cocoa
2 c. sugar
2 tbsp. corn syrup
2/3 c. milk or cream
2 tbsp. butter
1 tsp. vanilla
1/2 tsp. baking powder

Cut up chocolate (or use cocoa), and put into a saucepan with sugar, corn syrup, and milk. Stirring constantly, heat mixture until sugar dissolves. Continue cooking, stirring frequently, until temperature reaches 230° F. (or when a bit of the mixture forms a soft ball if dropped in cold water).

At this point, remove from heat, and add butter. Cool to lukewarm (110° F.). Add vanilla and baking powder, then beat until creamy, thick, and non-glossy. Pour into a greased 8-inch square pan. Cool and cut into squares.

Mary's Candied Grapefruit Peel
(Henry's Mother's Instructions)

Cut grapefruit peel (orange peel may also be used) into strips, and put into a saucepan. Cover with cold water and bring to a boil; reduce heat. Simmer, uncovered, for 10 minutes. Drain; then squeeze out the peel as dry as you can get it. Repeat — boiling, simmering, draining, and squeezing — five more times. (This is necessary to keep the resulting sweetmeats from tasting bitter and strong.)

Measure the amount of peel you have, put back into the saucepan, and add an equal amount of sugar. Cover with cold water. Boil until the water is absorbed, stirring occasionally. (As the amount of water lessens, watch carefully so as not to scorch the peel. — Stir gently, in order not to break the strips.)

Place the strips into a colander or on a wire rack to drain. (Put wax paper underneath.) As soon as the grapefruit peel can be handled, roll it in granulated sugar. Arrange the strips of sugar-coated peeling on waxed paper in a single layer to dry. (The strips can be shaped any way you wish.) Let dry overnight, and then store in an airtight container in the refrigerator. (It keeps indefinitely in the freezer.)

Results from the Yuletide survey reflect that even among young Americans there is a passion for various forms of transportation. Questionnaire recipients' answers to the favorite gift question included Evangeline Jones's (of Danville, Virginia) response: "A red wagon." Many mention receiving trikes and bikes (and the thrill of pulling off the blankets which often covered those "vehicles"). New sleds (and accompanying snow) made a special Christmas for some of my respondents. (Howard Watlington, Pittsylvania County native, remembers with delight several white Christmases at which time he looked for reindeer tracks in the snow.)

Marietta Watson, Chicago native, spoke of the pleasure of receiving a specific porcelain horse figurine "as requested" at age 5 or 7; while Massachusetts child Jennifer Smith cherishes the Christmas she received her first real horse.

Jennifer also remembers a Christmas prior to which her father had been gravely ill. At Christmastime he was getting better, and Jennifer describes poignantly the sense of gratefulness she felt upon hearing him, after she had gone to bed on Christmas Eve, "Ho-ho-ho"-ing. Ann Carlson of Janesville, Wisconsin, had a similar experience as she was growing up: "My Dad had been injured and was in the hospital six months. He came home for Christmas Eve."

Other favorite material gifts which people catalogued could be arranged chronologically to give a little "history lesson" or time line of tangible consumer goods. My father-in-law, born in 1904, listed a wind-up top and a cap pistol as his most special gifts received as a boy; his nephew, Jess Carr, remembered his first long pants (clothing was frequently given). A beloved Teddy Bear was listed; and Linda Yeatts of Virginia Beach wrote about a doll with her own canopy bed; Faye Oakes Peery was thrilled to receive a Snow White watch. Tiny Tears dolls were popular and Lincoln Logs. California resident Joy Bolyanatz lists a phonograph which played one 78 rpm record at a time. Joseph Melton stated that his favorite Christmas was in 1975 when he and his wife Helen moved into their newly-constructed home. A piano, a tape recorder, and a microwave were also happily-received consumer goods. My personal favorite material gift received as a child at Christmas? — My own pet Thesaurus!*

The just-mentioned Helen E. Melton contributed the following two recipes.

Chocolate-Covered Mounds

1 box confectioners' sugar
14 oz. coconut
3/4 c. prepared instant mashed potatoes (omit butter when preparing)
1 tsp. vanilla or coconut flavoring

Mix the above ingredients and form into balls. Freeze. When the balls are frozen, dip each one into the following mixture:

1 bar paraffin wax
6 oz. semi-sweet chocolate morsels
6 oz. dark chocolate squares

Melt the wax and chocolates together in the top of a double boiler. Using a toothpick or long fork, dip each ball into the chocolate and then place on waxed paper. Let the balls cool and refrigerate until used.

Chocolate Nut Balls

2 boxes confectioners' sugar
2 sticks butter or margarine, melted
3 c. nuts, chopped
1 c. sweetened condensed milk

1 12-oz. pkg. chocolate chips
1 1/2 bars paraffin

Form balls by mixing the first four ingredients. Chill. Then melt the chocolate chips and paraffin in a double boiler. Dip in the candy balls to coat with chocolate. Place on wax paper to cool.

My question about giving gifts, and whether they were handmade or storebought, revealed that many more people bought gifts than made them. — Robert Henderson, my Orleans, Indiana, spokesperson, answered that particular question with great wisdom. He quoted his mother as having emphasized to him "That the gift was what was in my heart, not what was in my hand."

Janette Forbes Beaver of Gaston County, North Carolina, remembers that the Dutch tradition of the family's gathering together was important, "not gifts or receiving." Julia Folkers, of Norwegian descent, commented about growing up in Minnesota, "I was born in 1902 so in our area at that time we had none of the elaborate extras people have today. *Jesus' birth was central."* She went on to state that she did not believe in Santa Claus as a real person — he was just played by someone. Of all my questionnaire respondents Julia Folkers is the only one who was not taught the "Santa myth" as a young child. [By the way, Henry and I have never indoctrinated our children with the Santa myth either, but instead tell them about the historical figures of Jesus (of course!) and Saint Nicholas.]

Most of the people who filled in my questionnaire wrote that they believed in a flying-sleigh-type of Santa Claus until they were 6 or 7 years old, but some did not find out the truth until they were 10 or 11. Sister Olivia Wassmer admitted that she *"knew better"* than to believe in the Santa Claus story "by age 6 but figured [she] would get more toys if [she] went along with the Santa Claus idea." Ron Smith, from Newport News, Virginia, recalls his favorite Christmas: ". . . 1961 or 1962. I knew of Santa's identity but my sisters did not. What fun being in on the conspiracy!!!"

A recent **New York Times** poll revealed that 96% of three-to-five-year-old children believe that Santa is a genuine person. Even among nine- and ten-year-olds, children who believe in Santa Claus outnumber nonbelievers by more than 2 to 1.

Robert Henderson's wise mama had a good thought concerning the legend of Santa Claus which tends to remove Santa from the tinsel and commercialism so often associated with him. She shared this philosophy with Robert in later years, saying that she felt that *"Santa"* was the spirit of giving in one's heart.

Fletcher Mormann, born in Baltimore, Maryland, describes his favorite Christmas in this manner: "[When I was] age 4 or 5 . . . some of the relatives visited on Christmas Eve, and one of my uncles dressed as Santa Claus — whom we recognized at once [as being the uncle]!"

Mary Ellen Mormann, Fletcher's wife, a Pittsylvania County, Virginia native, remembers that people in her community gathered in the fall for taffy pulls after the *sorghum molasses was made. Sticky sweet sorghum syrup was used in making candy which was then "pulled." (Trubie Mitchell, my father-in-law, recalls that "you'd get your 'best girl' to pull taffy with you . . . .") The children also helped at the gatherings, Mary Ellen recollects, and lots of the candy was put into jars to be brought out later as Christmas treats for the kids, that being "the only kind of candy we had."*

Molasses Taffy

1 c. molasses
1 c. sugar
1 tbsp. vinegar
1 tbsp. butter
1/8 tsp. baking soda

Put all ingredients except the baking soda into a pot. Cook slowly, stirring occasionally until the mixture reaches the hard ball stage. (A little bit of the syrup will form a ball when dropped into a glass of water. The ball would be hard enough to clink against the side of the glass.) Just before removing the taffy mixture from the stove, add the baking soda. Pour the candy into a buttered pan and let it cool enough to handle. Butter hands and pull the taffy until it is light. Shape into a rope and cut in short sections with scissors. Wrap the individual pieces in plastic wrap or waxed paper.

In 1223 in Italy, St. Francis of Assisi set up the first manger scene. He invited people to gather there to SING the gospel (and some of those ancient carols are still sung). — Numerous individuals who completed my inquiry form mentioned the manger scene or creche as being the focal point of their holiday decorations. Sister Olivia Wassmer describes a large creche, covering the entire dining room table. John Calabrisi tells about a ceramic creche displayed under the tree. He reminisces, "My mother would have a vigil candle lit under the tree in the manger for days before Christmas, and after midnight it was put out [because] at midnight our parents would put the Infant Child [figure] in the manger."

Jennifer Smith tells about an ongoing Christmas tradition: "Moving Mary and Joseph around the room each morning until Christmas Eve when they arrive at the nativity scene." (Also, on every Christmas Eve, Jennifer's family stands in a circle, holding hands, and sings Christmas carols.)

My survey clearly showed differences in thinking about holiday traditions. One person, answering the "creche question" said that "My father felt that they were 'graven images;' and that you would tend to think more of the symbols than what they stand for, and forget the spiritual aspect of Christmas."

On the affirmative side, Ann Miller, native of North Carolina, comments on the favorite manger scene in her beautiful collection of Christmas decorations — a creche from Oberammergau that was given to her. Linda Yeatts, originally from Chatham, describes a rustic, wooden-style manger scene made in Germany. Hidden within the stable is a music box. Others mentioned a handmade porcelain scene, a plastic one, an appliqued manger scene; ceramic and papier-mâché manger scenes were also reported. Families treasure their creches, often owning very old ones regarded as heirlooms.

In the past, not so very long ago, many children were thankful to receive some oranges and candy in their stocking; and perhaps, if they were really blessed, to be given a new (and needed) garment to wear. My father used to describe his Christmases as being (according to the current very commercial/materialistic approach to the holiday) rather Spartan. — In a house with five boys, a stocking and some clothes were enough of a capital outlay! My mother recalls receiving a bit more in the way of gifts, but she, too, recalls the special fruits found in her stocking. Her childhood favorite? Sugar plums (large dark raisins still on the stems in a bunch).

Another Christmas fruit treat popular in this area is an orange with a peppermint stick or cane stuck in one end. The child (or adult) enjoying this delicacy sort of licks/sucks/eats the candy cane, simultaneously slurping up some of the orange juice. (My Daddy taught me this sticky and refreshing "recipe!")

Eleanor Haskins, a Chatham, Virginia friend wrote about an old local custom which I, too, recalled when I read her questionnaire. "Our church, Green Pond [Baptist]," she says, "always gave everyone a brown paper bag with an orange, apple, walnuts in the shell, and some candy. [It] was a treat to us."

"Visions of Sugar Plums" Nut Roll

The following instructions for "Visions of Sugar Plums" Nut Roll were given to me by Helen Melton. Her great-aunt, Carrie Alley, gave her the recipe (and so it goes with commendable recipes: they are transferred from place to place and generation to generation . . .). Although this nut roll does not contain sugar plums, *per se*, it does feature raisins and many other "sweet-tooth-satisfiers." Perhaps you, too, will night dream (or daydream) of this holiday pleasure.

* * *

8 oz. candied pineapple
1 (1-lb.) box graham crackers, finely crushed
1 small jar maraschino cherries, drained
1 can angel flake coconut
1 box golden seedless raisins
1 lg. pkg. miniature marshmallows
1 can Eagle Brand sweetened condensed milk
1 lb. pecans (before cracking)
1 lb. English walnuts (before cracking)

Have nuts and all ingredients ready before starting to make the roll. Save out about 3/4 to 1 cup of graham cracker crumbs to roll the dough in. Heat milk on low heat, just warm enough to dissolve the marshmallows (do not let milk boil). Have all other ingredients ready in a large mixing bowl. You must use your hands to mix. Leave cherries whole; break nuts into large pieces. Mix all well. Divide the dough into three parts, and form a roll from each part, using the cracker crumbs you saved to roll them in to keep them from sticking to your hands. After shaping each roll, put it in wax paper or freezer paper and store in refrigerator. The rolls will keep two or three weeks. Slice to serve.

Note: The milk used is sweet and thick and easy to stick to your pan as you melt the marshmallows; so you need to watch it carefully.

Ann Miller, who grew up in Hillsborough, North Carolina, shares a touching "Depression Christmas" memory with us, plus a festive candy recipe (Ann's mother operated a kindergarten at her home.)

My Favorite Christmas Present

"When I came home from school for Christmas vacations, my mother was usually still teaching for several days before her holiday began. She always wanted me to visit her class for the final day party. I loved helping her hand out refreshments and gifts, and the children thought it was really special to have a visitor. One year, during the Depression, after all had received gifts and treats, one darling little freckled-face girl named Maggie noticed that I was the only one not receiving a gift and called me over to her desk. She had evidently received a package of chewing gum and was chomping away joyfully. Each stick was wrapped in pink paper. She popped a new stick into her mouth, bit it in two, wrapped it, tooth *marks and all, in the nice pink paper, and presented it to me, beaming and awaiting my thankful response. I've never forgotten this sweet sharing, for Maggie, I'm sure, did not have many treats given her."*

Home for the Holidays Christmas Strawberries

One special holiday memory of mine involves receiving an annual gift box of (to me) exotic fruits from a sophisticated and rather well-off aunt and uncle. This gift to our family included different fruits attractively wrapped in light green tissue paper. Unwrapping unknown fruits like kumquats was very exciting to me. Nowadays one could, I suppose, purchase strawberries in December in this country, but back then even the fancy fruit boxes did not contain such rarities. So? Make 'em yourself!

* * *

1 can Borden's sweetened condensed milk
1/2 lb. fine coconut (or 7-oz. pkg.)
1/2 lb. almonds, finely chopped
2 pkgs. strawberry Jello, used dry
1 tsp. vanilla
A few drops of red coloring
1 tsp. red crystal sugar

Mix all together well. Save out enough almonds, slim cut, for green stems. (Soak in green coloring.) Let candy mixture stand in refrigerator for 12 hours. Shape into "strawberries." Makes 100, depending on size.

In Scandinavia it is believed that you will have "good luck" if birds live on your land. (Birds are certainly a pretty sight; and a boon to gardeners, because our feathery friends eat so many insects.) In order to attract more birds the

Scandinavians "decorate" an outdoor Christmas tree for the birds. (They also have an indoor tree.)

   If you wish to start this tradition, select an evergreen, and hang on it suet and seeds. Birds also like peanut butter. Hollowed-out gourds make handy containers for this purpose. Indian corn, and thin short strings of raisins, popcorn, and cranberries are appropriate goodies. (Use the thin, short pieces of string to avoid the possibility of a bird or small animal's becoming entangled.) Sheaves of grain tied together with red ribbon look jolly on the tree. — To attract larger species of wildlife, nuts, apples, carrots, crackers, and cheese can be scattered near the base of the tree. Replenish the food as it is eaten, and you may be rewarded with the sight of squirrels, chipmunks, raccoons, foxes, rabbits, deer, and game birds, as well as the more typical wild birds.

   When I was a child I occasionally decorated a small cedar for the birds, especially if it was a snowy or drear December. It was fun to watch the birds peck at the tidbits, and to feel that I was sharing the joy of Christ's birth with some of God's creatures.

Peanut Butter Candy

   Just as surely as standing under a sprig of berry-laden mistletoe makes me want to pucker up, the earthy smell of peanut butter makes me eager to "chow down!" If, while putting out peanut butter, etc., for the wildlife, the aroma of this high-protein spread gets to you, prepare the following sweet indulgence! (The recipe is provided compliments of Nancy Johnson Sharp of Hillsville, Virginia.)

* * *

1 stick margarine, melted
1 box confectioners' sugar
2 tbsp. milk
Peanut butter

Add the melted margarine to the confectioners' sugar. Pour 2 tbsp. milk into the mixture. Mix all together (add more confectioners' sugar, if needed).

Divide the dough into four pieces and roll out into rectangles. Spread peanut butter on the rectangles and roll them up. Chill and slice.

Decorations for Christmas seem to have become more elaborate in this day and age (although the Victorian era certainly had its "finery")! Finances also, of course, play a part in how a family decorates for the holidays. Natural greenery has long been popular: mistletoe, holly, running cedar, a tree, wreaths. Older people remember decorating their tree with handmade paper loops and popcorn strings. (My more northern respondents remember cranberry strings.) Some got a little fancier, as did Eleanor Mullins, by using colored glass, balls, tinsel, the popcorn strings, candy canes, a star, and candles. She remarks, "The candles were lit only at special times. Daddy had a bucket of water close by."

Sister Olivia Wassmer shares an Indiana memory with us: "My last Christmas before entering the monastery [*was her favorite Christmas remembered*]. We had a gorgeous tree, from floor to ceiling and for the first time it seemed that there were enough lights. (Almost every year I would say I'd like to have more lights on the tree.)"

She goes on: "When I was small (lower grades), we would go out to Grandma's during the holidays, and they always had a small fir tree for me, not more than two feet high, and decorated with candies that were made to hang on a Christmas tree. They cut it from their own woods, and had it on a stand. It was mine to take home. Those candies for hanging were always a part of Christmas, too."

Marie Wells's Date Roll

Stuart Wells, our journalist friend who grew up in Greenville, North Carolina, mentioned, as I said earlier, the heady fragrance of fir trees as being associated with his Christmas memories; and "trimming the tree" as being a special family activity. — Another Christmas morning highlight at Stuart's house? A pancake breakfast prepared by his dad! One of Stuart's most favorite treats is his Mom's date roll, and I'm sure he would also love Carrie Alley's Holiday World Date Swirls, a recipe for which is found after this recipe.

* * *

1 stick butter or margarine
1 c. sugar
1 pkg. dates, finely chopped
1 egg, beaten

3 c. Rice Krispies
Shredded coconut

Mix together the first four ingredients in a pot and heat until warm and melty. Cook 5 minutes, or until thickened. Stir in the Rice Krispies. Allow to cool. Shape into a log and roll in coconut. Slice to serve.

Holiday World Date Swirls

1/2 lb. pitted dates, cut up
1/4 c. sugar
1/3 c. water
1 tbsp. lemon juice
3/4 c. chopped pecans

Combine the first four ingredients. Cook over medium heat about 5 minutes, stirring often. Add pecans and set aside to cool.

Cream together:

1/2 c. margarine or Crisco
1 tsp. pure vanilla
1/2 c. white sugar and 1/2 c. brown sugar
1 egg
1/2 tsp. baking soda and 1/2 tsp. salt
2 c. plain flour

Mix well. Divide dough into four parts. Put flour on board and roll each portion about as thin as sugar cookie dough and spread date-nut mixture evenly to all edges. Roll up. Wrap in wax paper and lay on cookie sheet. Put rolls into refrigerator and chill for at least 6 hours. When ready to bake, turn oven to 325° F. Using a sharp knife, slice rolls off (about 1/8 - 1/4 inch thick) and bake on cookie sheet just until light brown. Leave space between the pieces; they rise some while baking.

Grandma's Cookies

Epps Perrow, talented local artist and cook, gave me this recipe.

* * *

1 c. white granulated sugar
1 c. brown sugar
1 c. shortening
3 eggs
2 tsp. vanilla
(Chocolate bits, nuts, raisins if desired)
2 c. quick-cooking oatmeal
2 c. flour
1 tsp. baking soda
1 tsp. baking powder
1 tsp. salt
2 c. Rice Crispies

Cream sugars and shortening. Add beaten eggs and vanilla. Mix dry ingredients with this. Mix well. Drop by teaspoonfuls on lightly-greased cookie sheets. Bake 12-15 minutes at 350° F.

Chocolate Nut-Crackle Sauce

And the grand finale recipe, also compliments of Epps Perrow:

* * *

1/2 stick butter
1 c. nuts, chopped
Pinch of salt

6 oz. semi-sweet block chocolate

Cook together the first three ingredients over low heat until light golden brown. Remove from heat and stir in chocolate. Refrigerate. When ready to serve reheat over hot water.

Serve over vanilla ice cream.

Amid all of the cooking, shopping, wrapping, and bustling about we all need to remember that Christmas is truly a birthday celebration! One year this point was particularly brought home to me when on a wintery December night I was sitting in the bedroom holding our newborn first baby, Sarah Evangeline, and a group of Christmas carolers from the church appeared beneath the window, singing lovely songs telling of the birth of Jesus. The candles which they were holding revealed the love in their faces; their sweet voices told of the awe and joy of visiting a new baby. With a sense of deep reverence in my heart, I felt a kinship to the mother of our Lord.